2012
AND
BEYOND

Archangel Michael

2012
AND BEYOND:

THE TRUTH
from
Archangel Michael

Kelly Hampton

Editing by WordSharp.net

BALBOA.
PRESS

Also by Kelly Hampton
Books

Into the White Light: The Revelations of Archangel Michael

Available upon request at your local bookstore, Amazon.com,
Scribd.com or www.intothewhitelight.com

Balboa Press books may be ordered through booksellers or by contacting:

Balboa Press
A Division of Hay House
1663 Liberty Drive
Bloomington, IN 47403
www.balboapress.com
1-(877) 407-4847

Because of the dynamic nature of the Internet, any Web addresses or links contained in
this book may have changed since publication and may no longer be valid. The views
expressed in this work are solely those of the author and do not necessarily reflect the
views of the publisher, and the publisher hereby disclaims any responsibility for them.

ISBN: 978-1-4525-0095-9 (sc)
ISBN: 978-1-4525-0097-3 (e)

Library of Congress Control Number: 2010915352

The author of this book does not dispense medical advice or prescribe the use of any
technique as a form of treatment for physical, emotional, or medical problems without the
advice of a physician, either directly or indirectly. The intent of the author is only to offer
information of a general nature to help you in your quest for emotional and spiritual well-
being. In the event you use any of the information in this book for yourself, which is your
constitutional right, the author and the publisher assume no responsibility for your actions.

Printed in the United States of America

Balboa Press rev. date: 10/18/2010

*This book is dedicated to everyone who
assisted me during its creation,
including those who provided editorial and dictation services,
thought-provoking questions posed to Archangel Michael,
and those who offered moral support in
seeing the book's completion.
To Hay House,
for the creation of Balboa Press,
allowing unrepresented authors
with important spiritual messages
to spread them throughout the world.*

*Most importantly,
I offer my heartfelt appreciation
to Archangel Michael, my friend, my guide,
my inspiration,
for asking me to be the messenger of love and kindness.
I hope that I have served you well.
I am looking forward with anticipation
to your next book of wisdom.*

Contents

*A*uthor's Note

By now, it should come as no surprise to me that I am a messenger of the divine realm, specifically for now, channeling Archangel Michael. He was the source for my first book, ***Into The White Light: The Revelations of Archangel Michael*** and now this one. He is the source who continues to guide souls through my personal consultations on a daily basis and he is the one who gifted me with a new healing modality to teach and share with the world in January 2010. Archangel Michael has asked me to call this new modality Star Healing Intergalactic Energy for the Ascension, which is the period we are living in now and leading up to 2012 and beyond.

What does continue to surprise me is the clarity of the wisdom, the beauty I find in it and how divinely wise it is to my ears. Some readers may continue to question what is contained in the following pages and I am good with all of this. It is diversity that creates and enriches our world. I wait in anticipation for the next revelation from the Angel to share with the world. In summary, be blessed, be open to receiving good, be kind and loving. The best is yet to come.

INTRODUCTION

Speaking of the Cosmos

If your eyes are reading this text, and I know for most of you around the world that your eyes will be reading this text before 2012, I believe it is important to imagine what that world will be like. From your vantage point, dear souls, wherever you may be, I ask you to begin imagining the world in 2012. Is it a world filled with fear or hope? Are you imagining a world near destruction or rebirth? I intend to share my divine wisdom to help paint the real picture. In order to do that, it is important for mankind to reflect upon certain things. The messages I convey are global in nature; they are everlasting in their truth and they will undeniably be questioned before I am finished.

Like a loving father, I will be striving for a relationship with my children, you my children, based on trust. Some will be like rebellious children, and will find what I say irritating, and others will find my wisdom profound. It makes no difference to me where you stand. Now let us begin.

Before humanity existed on the Earth plane, before mankind existed on Earth in your reality, I say to you, mankind was first created in a distant galaxy. The distant galaxy is known as the Pleiadian Galaxy. There are over sixteen galaxies in the universes of which I will speak. Your galaxy is one, the Pleiadian Galaxy is another, and you may view the remaining galaxies as if you are putting ingredients into a cake in which all of its ingredients make up one total reality.

The Pleiadian Galaxy has existed before creation. I know this will fall upon some ears as simply untrue. I expect this and I honor this. It is important to realize this one beginning truth before we continue, and the truth stated another way is that mankind's galaxy is not the only galaxy supporting life. It is important to understand this concept so that you can move your ego aside and understand that for many of you your original home can simply not be called Mother Earth. I do indeed want to assure you that this communication together, this information together, is one of collective divine wisdom.

By that, I mean, it is not simply my version of the truth; it is the version of every being from the angelic realm. I would also like to take the opportunity to let every soul know in advance, it is not my intent to frighten, alarm, or dissuade anyone being from a place of harmony. I would agree, sometimes truth can be frightening, but this is not a book about the end of the world, it is wisdom about the *creation* of the world. With that in mind, I invite you to cast aside certain beliefs you may have already formed in your mind about 2012 and the years beyond it and start afresh. Lastly, I am asking everyone, when finished reading this material, to embrace their brother and sister with new eyes, and what are the 'new eyes'? Eyes possessing a greater depth of love and kindness, compassion, hope…acceptance. Sit back, strap yourself into the intergalactic starship and get ready for a heck of a ride.

1

2012 What Does It Hold?

I am trying to decide how to share this information for your understanding and not sound like an astrophysicist, but share some principles of great science. With this in mind, I invite the most enlightened earthly figures of the world as well as those souls very young of the mind, to embark on this journey with me. The journey right now is this: between this moment and 2012 there are going to be a series of seismic eruptions. This in and of itself is not that unusual, because mankind has experienced seismic eruptions throughout history. If I were to tell you that the seismic eruptions to come are being caused by interstellar influences, this may be a surprise. It is what will happen. Let me state this more clearly: there are other dimensions with a greater intelligence than your own. You may be asking yourselves, "Then what is the purpose of earthly eruptions from another dimension? Especially if you say, Angel, that those of the other galaxy are more intelligent than we are?" And I say to you, the reason for this series of eruptions is so the toxins that are contained within Mother Earth, which are thoughts that have been created over your history, are released.

Returning to something that I just said, and that is, other life forms of intelligences, dozens actually, exist outside of your world. Remember, I began by stating that this is how the majority of you came here to Earth from the Pleiadian Galaxy. By now already, I suppose many of you are scoffing at the idea. Again, this is not new to me, I love each and every one of you whether you believe my wisdom or not. To continue, this is actually seen as a great blessing, this higher form of intelligence. For without it, I suggest that many of the great accomplishments in your earthly history would not have occurred. Without your origins developing from a higher intelligence, mankind's economic, spiritual and physical development would have been thwarted (halted).

Now, I would like to share the wisdom of Herculan with you, (not the carpeting familiar to some of you). Herculan is another galaxy in which intelligent life exists. Some of the stars of the Pleiadian galaxy can be seen with the naked eye depending upon which part of the world you are viewing the sky from, unlike Herculan, which is thousands of thousands of light years away. Herculan cannot be seen by the naked eye; nevertheless, Herculan exists and is another galaxy I would like you to become familiar with. Herculan is a galaxy comprised of several planets. Their collective energy is one of strength and power and it is funny to me in a way that a Herculan fiber is indicative of the Herculan Galaxy in its strength and durability. So the next time you may walk upon your carpeting for those that have it, think of this intelligent life in a far off distant galaxy. Since this is a document of 2012 and beyond, it is important to know that the Herculan Galaxy, of which Herculan is a major planet, will be discovered in the next one hundred years. Interstellar travel between your galaxy and the Herculan Galaxy will occur within three hundred years.

Why is this important to know?

It is every bit as important to know as any other of your earthly discoveries have been. It will be a discovery of monumental proportions likened to the discovery that your world is not flat by Galileo, the infamous sixteenth century astronomer. This will be seen as THE discovery of the new frontier.

Interstellar communication is going to involve travel; travelling between your world and other galaxies. This is going to occur in the next generation's lifetime. There is likely to be some global trepidation unless the truth of interstellar life is presented in a non-threatening way. Part of the *meaning* behind 2012 is this opening of the doorway from your world to others. Please promise me, dear souls, that you will not make fun of the little green Martians because they do not exist. What does exist is a loving, infinitely expansive cosmic tapestry. You might say that the purpose of the changes, the shifting of the energies, which are already being felt in your world by light workers, is in preparation for the launching of interstellar communication as never before witnessed. By now, your minds may be questioning me, may be questioning God. I say to you that what I have said so far does nothing to diminish the power of belief in the existent of God, the God Force, and the Infinite Mind. I have not said that there are twelve Gods or twelve Infinite Minds, have I? I have simply said that there are multi-galaxies and therefore multi-dimensions.

Does anyone know what a star-seed is? I would like to enlighten. A star-seed is someone who came to Earth from either the Pleiadian Galaxy or Herculan Galaxy, with the purpose of transmuting any disharmonies. I suppose that is almost too broad to imagine so I will clarify for your minds. A star-seed, for example, might be someone sitting across the table from you, but their soul essence came for the expressed purpose of facilitating a smooth transference of Earth energy to intergalactic energy. You might think of a star-seed, as someone like a CEO who is put in a position to oversee a job and to ensure that the job of others is done smoothly. It is not important that you recognize a star-seed because in every way, shape, and fashion they look like you, they, or them. It is important to know that they exist to help understand that there is a Divine Intelligence, a Divine Mind that orchestrates everything that goes on in your world, everything, absolutely everything.

Q. Are we headed for earthly catastrophes like earthquakes and polar shifts?

A: Yes, I will honor that the Earth will be adapting to some cosmic changes, but the Earth and other planets always have. They simply change form. Your planet, your home is not going to crumble away. Currently, the polar shift is already happening. Currently, your planet is already experiencing earthquakes. My vision is not to produce fear. There is more to say about this but I will end here for now to allow you to absorb this wisdom.

I would like to quell some of the fears of 2012 and the Mayan calendar, the prophecies of the Mayan calendar. Let me restate, that while there may be some eruptions within Mother Earth between now and 2012 Mother Earth is going to be reborn, will be re-birthed. Let me reassure those who are living in fear that 2012 signifies the end of the world; your fears are simply unfounded. Recall, I stated that change can make people feel uncomfortable (it is necessary of soul growth). Yes, Mother Earth will change but she will not collapse. She will not disintegrate into some ball of fire or implode upon herself. What is true of part of the Mayan 2012 philosophies is in recognizing that there will be some earthly disruptions. So I say, do not fear this time; do not horde water, food, provisions. Everything, I say in that sense, will be given to you and more. What is happening already is a shift in consciousness, and the shift in consciousness is really a reaction. It is a result of the changes in the Earth's rotation. The changing in consciousness, the changing of the vibration's consciousness happening now and through 2012 is a cosmic one. It's a reaction like a ripple. What is the stone that made the ripple? It is the increasing velocity of the rotation of the Earth.

It is a bit like this – if your mind is wondering, why is this happening? I will say to you, the Divine Mind, the Infinite Mind actually has a divine plan. The plan is this; Mother Earth spins faster now than she ever has before (There are male and female energies). It is an attempt to raise global awareness so that no one remains in the same vibration that they entered with.

This is a powerfully divine holy matter, no matter what your religion, no matter what your culture. Let me give an example to illustrate this point. I am aware that some children play a game called 'crack the whip.' This game is where children are lined up hand-in-hand, and they run and pull each other like a snake. The leader of the line can make the line go faster or slower. The faster the line, the harder it is for the children at the end to keep their grasp. Eventually the last few children usually fall off unharmed by the velocity of the whipping action of the game. So it is very much like the increasing velocity of the world you live in, as the vibration speeds up, the rotation speeds up, and the lower frequencies get dropped to the ground like the children. Lower frequencies are things like hatred, deception, treachery and so on. What other wisdom other than the Divine Mind could have created something as miraculously beautiful as this?

Think of it this way on more practical terms, that the infinite Cosmic Mind, God, God-force is shaking Mother Earth in a gentle way, in a gently loving way. You might say shaking her like a newborn baby as it wakes up to the promise of a new world, where souls see the world with new eyes, because their eyes will be made new. This is starting to be done already with the light workers of the world. They, you might say, are the gatekeepers holding the gates open to higher frequencies of thinking, being and living, so that everyone may follow and walk through. This is what is going to happen between now and 2012.

Q: Is this going to be the year for the second coming? And if not, will we see the second coming ourselves?

A: To which second coming are you referring to, the second coming of my Master, yes. The second coming of your own spiritual rebirth, yes; the second coming of the New World Order, yes.

Now a lesson in science for those unaccustomed, here I become the scientist. For those unacquainted with frequency and vibration to understand the importance of what was just stated more fully, please allow me to educate. Everything in your world, in your dimension, is a vibration.

Every object, every thought is a vibration. Every vibration translates into a frequency. Many can appreciate the Hertz frequency, so when I say to you that 2012 is a time when lower frequencies will be banished, I mean the emotions associated with negativity, which carry a very low or slow vibration. I, on the other hand, often reside in the fifth dimension, a dimension of pure love and oneness. My frequency and that of those in my dimension, only carry this vibration, so it is the Infinite Mind working, creating an opportunity in time for your fourth dimension to rise to the fifth dimension.

I would like to pose a couple of questions for your reflection. Who do you think carries the highest vibration: a man who has just lost his job or a man who has just secured a new job? The simplest of answers as the mind thinks them, is that the man who just secured the new job resonates at a higher frequency, because he most likely embodies emotions like joy, excitement, hope, anticipation and gratitude. But, if we extend the learning further, I will suggest to you that this soul could also simultaneously possess the lower vibrations of the two men. How so? The man with the new position could also carry frequencies that resonate with fear, doubt, uncertainty, and worry. So you see, the discussion of frequency, vibration and resonance can be a very complicated matter indeed.

Q: Why is this important, Angel, that we understand the meaning of 2012 and beyond?

A: It is important to understand when someone asks you what 2012 is about, as I am trying to explain is, there is not one single answer, not one single frequency. So, I say to you, some souls around the world even within their own homes and villages will simultaneously carry high vibrational energy and low vibrational energy as they think about 2012. It is my desire that this material, that this wisdom, enlightens those in their homes and villages, so that once and for all they may shift aside the low vibrations, so the only things that remain are, love, kindness, compassion, forgiveness and non-judgment.

If I were to tell you, that many of Indigo and Crystalline Children who have already entered your world have a new DNA structure within them that actually prevents judgment from forming, how would you respond to this? I will tell you how the divine realm is responding to this. We are in celebration! If you can imagine a billion angels all jumping up and down at one time, then you will imagine this well. I would like to make two points here for pause and reflection—

1. The concept of life without judgment and
2. The concept of angels jumping up and down

If I have enlisted a chuckle, then I will have affected your vibration. That being said, it does not take an angel to affect your vibration.

Imagine now, the depth and Infinite Wisdom that created this time in your world that is unlike any other. The point worth reflecting upon is the concept that souls in your world today under the age of ten and all of the souls of their children, in other words all generations of those souls, have genetically been reconstructed to live lives without judgment. How huge, how beautiful, how graceful this gift!

To demonstrate further, I would ask everyone to list for me and for themselves ten things they regularly judge in their lives. I will make a few suggestions to get your minds going—judging someone by their appearance, judging someone by their vocation, making moral judgments and I would also say placing judgment upon yourself.

If you happen to be fortunate enough to have met any of the Crystalline Children under the age of ten, you will notice something different about them when you met them but will not know what it is. I will tell you what it is: the removal of judgment from their soul. If you are fortunate enough to meet a Crystalline Child and be in their company for a few minutes, you will start witnessing different things, and one of the differences is that they will look at you differently than other people. How will they look at you differently you ask? Their eyes will have no judgment in them; it's like a filter that has been taken out. And since their eyes are a reflection of their soul, what you are likely to see and experience in this first round, this first generation of Crystalline Children, is unconditional love. I wonder how many of you have experienced unconditional love from a stranger, but this is what the Crystalline Children were asked to bring to your world.

I hear some of you saying, "Angel, but without judgment how will I know anything?" I say to you, it is not judgment that creates thought. It is the judgment that creates prejudice, jealousy, and greed. You see, in order for Mother Earth to have the high vibrational energy that 2012 is bringing to her, there has to be souls to support it, to root it to her. And there will be more and more and more every single day, until the year 2500, if your mind can imagine that.

Let us go back and examine the idea of judgment again. It is just one element; one thread of the 'New World Order' and the new world order is another way of saying it is the time of the Great Awakening. What is the Great Awakening? It is the great awakening of spiritual consciousness. It is actually a re-awakening of the known frequencies that exist and derive from the Pleiadian and Herculan galaxies. If you can imagine this in another way – imagine over the centuries that your world and all of its inhabitants evolved to develop a cloud or a fog over them, over the Earth. Then you will have envisioned exactly what has happened. Through the centuries mankind's thoughts collectively have clouded Mother Earth; because again, Mother Earth is a planet and a planet is a living thing just as the stars are living things, as asteroids are living things, as black holes are living things, and as solar flares are living things with a pulse and a tempo. If you are following my wisdom, you are beginning to understand that the cloud that has been created was actually created through judgment.

Q. Will the New World Order be in effect by then?

A: You ask some universally important questions as all questions are important to your universe. Perhaps some clarity about the phrase, 'New World Order' is in order? The New World Order is comprised of many things. It is comprised of a complex correlation between man, animal and God/Infinite Mind. If you think of the New World Order as this, then you will begin to understand the founding energies. This still, is large in nature to comprehend. The New World Order will come into existence by 2012 and it will continue for at least a thousand years thereafter. What is it then? As spoken of in many of your texts, it is a time of salvation. To this, I would agree. It is not, however, as in some texts and propagations, the Armageddon—the end of the world. The New World Order is an overthrow around the globe of all of those manmade 'things,' 'constructs,' and 'conventions' that are run by ill minds by ill formed desires.

Imagine the fog lifting and you will imagine the reality that each of you will be stepping into in 2012. Up until 2012, it may be said that the divine minds of the multi-universes are getting your Earth ready. It's a bit like an athlete warming up a muscle before going into practice. What great wisdom there is in this! One more exercise about judgment, before we leave this topic. You may do it if you wish for soul growth. I ask you to take a week out of your lives and keep track of how many times you make a judgment about something during the course of your day. Most of you will be amazed by the number of times you form a judgment. One last thing: you may say, "Angel, I do not understand the value of this restructuring, the renewing power of this new DNA without judgment in it? Help me to understand this further."

You may be saying that judgment helps me to make wise decisions. I say to you that this is simply untrue. Try this experiment: tie a cloth around your eyes for a day and go about you lives in this manner. Sadly, judgment has become largely a visual one. If I told you that people without sight were some of the most enlightened teachers of your world, what would you say? The next time you see a blind person on the street I ask you to bless them and thank them for teaching you non-judgment.

Crystalline Children are actually known by this name in some regions of your world. They received their name Crystalline Children by the crystalline frequency they carry. The crystalline frequency originates in the Pleiadian and Herculan galaxies; the Crystalline Children, in addition to having their molecular structure changed so they can enter your world without judgment, possess an insatiable curiosity, an insatiable calmness and peace. At first, they may seem to be strange, and indeed, they are different from the majority of the souls in your world today. However, by 2012 they, along with the Indigo Children, the Rainbow Children, and the Atlantean (Atlantis) Children will be approaching the majority.

> *Give thanks, now it is your turn to jump up and down.*
> *You may think of them as the genetic blueprint for the Earth.*
> *Hallelujah! Rejoice!*

Let me go on to say, that in no way, shape or fashion is it my intent for anyone who is reading these words or listening to this wisdom, to feel guilty for the thoughts of themselves or their ancestors of the creation of this cloud. You see, frequency along with judgment is being moved aside. I offered this just as an explanation of what is going on and why. You can, however, even without being a light-worker or one of the enlightened younger generations, take up your own sword and join in the unseen spiritual army where light overcomes darkness. Because you see, if the Crystalline Children and others like them are seen as the generals in this 'unseen army' they need troops to support them. Please be clear with this in your mind, when you think and say, the word 'sword' it is a sword that can only heal with divine light.

As 2012 approaches and subsequently in the immediate time past 2012, as a result of these shifting, renewing, globally conscious energies, there will be less war, less famine, less hatred, less poverty, fewer diseases. When you read about, when you hear conjecture and speculation about 2012 and beyond, which says that the world is coming to an end, I would agree to that with this point of distinction: the world *as you know it* is coming to an end.

Before I go on, I wish to give my thanks to those light workers who have made themselves available for this transformation to take place and there are millions of you in existence now. If I said to you that every light-worker reading this text or hearing these words, have known in their souls since birth that they would be assisting in this at this time in mankind's history; this may surprise you also. I hope that my surprises are seen more like positive enlightenment rather than startling and unsettling. Without the light workers who have been called to serve, who have agreed to serve, there would be some large cosmic obstructions. Some of the large cosmic obstructions of which I speak are life forms in other galaxies not fully in the light. As you know, there is lightness and darkness in your own lives, so it should be easy to extend the concept that there is goodness and darkness in other galaxies.

Therefore, a pledge to serve in the light-worker's army:

"I _____, agree to serve in the Unseen Spiritual Army

Of the Great Awakening.

When a soul agrees to this, it is a spiritual commitment that they will demonstrate love and kindness in some way until they cross over and leave the Earth plane of existence. To give an example, it could mean that when a soul is old and grey they remember to open a door for someone, smile to a neighbor. You see, in that sense, love has no boundary, love has no value. Be taught, that the frequency of a smile has as much frequency as the intent of a hundred people reconstructing a town after a flood. I am personally assigning certain specific jobs to assist with integration of the 2012 energies. By that, I mean, for a soul who wishes to do more (this has been happening to tens of thousands of souls) I will humbly advise them, assign them to a particular area of the world to work in. For some souls who wish to sign the service agreement, it may involve sending healing energy through the mind thousands of miles away to where that person may be living. That is, of course, the power of the mind. I have, for example, already called dozens to serve in Pakistan through mind healing. I have already called thousands to serve in Ethiopia through mind healing. I have already called thousands of light workers to send healing energy to

Belfast. There are noticeably certain regions of your world, Mother Earth, that have been more damaged by mankind's thoughts throughout the centuries than others have.

I have the greatest job in the universes, for I get to work with this gigantic crossword puzzle, filling in the blanks with the pieces that need to be put in place. These areas mentioned are by no means the only areas that need service from those in my spiritual army. Please make sure that when I use these words and you think of words like 'army' and 'soldier,' you begin to dissolve any images and thoughts you may have associated with these two words that invoke any images of killing or destruction. Replace in your mind, in your cell memories therefore, that the army I am talking about is the army of love. When you are drawn to sign this document, you can choose your own backyard if you wish in which to serve or you may call upon your Infinite God, Infinite Mind wisdom, and serve in the furthest corners of the globe. It is not terribly difficult for souls to identify in their own minds where in the world needs help. I am asking wherever in the world you think needs help, give it.

We have global markers in place, almost like a giant scorecard of what quadrants of the globe are receiving greater healing than others; because thought is an energy that can be measured. Since land is denser than water, my preference is that those who need more direction on where to serve and where to send their healing energy should choose a land-mass first. When I say dense, it means that land mass retains more memory than water mass. To further this idea, I say to you that when there is a flood, the water, which floods the land, is actually cleansing it.

Q. Can Archangel Michael advise us on how to stop animal cruelty and will it end by 2012?

A: There will be many alternative energies entering in the next five years, which will help right this cruelty. The vibration of cruelty is being torn apart with every loving, gentle thought and action. How to stop it? Believe it will stop and take positive action, sending loving energy to those who abuse and misuse.

Love has the power times one thousand...one million times the frequency of negativity. Grab hold of your inner wisdom, your inner glory, and honor each and every living thing.

It is in context that the density of the Earth and the idea that Earth has a memory, and that it is harder to remove or restore than water, than land, that gave germ warfare its roots to grow. Take a minute to let that sink into your consciousness. Some of you may or may not be familiar with germ warfare but let me say it this way. Because of the new rays—because that is what 2012 really is—ray energy—the new violet rays from these two magnificent galaxies, Pleiadian and Herculan, germ warfare will not exist any longer. Germ warfare was able to have a breeding ground for mankind's atrocities on Mother Earth. Which leads me to another topic: why, then, is Mother Earth having all of these horrible things happen to her? Why are all of these hurricanes, floods, tornadoes, tsunamis, seemingly happening with greater frequency? I say to you, without the inference of guilt straightforwardly, it was mankind's thoughts throughout time that opened up this door. I say to you, therefore, intelligence greater than your own has intervened.

Some of you who are entering this period view 2012 from the perspective that it is a time of Nirvana. The pendulum swings from those who fear 2012 and the years beyond to those who see it as a marvelous Nirvanic experience. Those who see it as a Nirvanic experience are resonating closer to the truth.

What can souls expect in 2011? They can expect friendships developing amongst strangers. They can expect varying degrees of physical ailments, which are temporary. There will be a restructuring of the world's financial centers and the plant and animal kingdom will continue to modify its molecular DNA structure. You can expect some reforestation; expect to learn of forests that will need to die in order for trees with new DNA to take their place. Until now, I have been talking about 'you,' the collective soul, 'you' the body, human. But, of course, that is only one form of life on your planet and since nothing exists in a vacuum, I would like to describe changes to expect within your plant and animal kingdom.

Perhaps I should have started a dialogue with the plant and animal kingdom, because in terms of hierarchy of life, it is equal to that of man. If I have upset some of you so much that you have closed this book or have turned off your ears, I honor this. But to those of you who are still engaged, I ask of you to accept this wisdom as truth. I think many of you will understand the idea this way. The level of divinity within the tiniest titmouse is the same as that of the mightiest sequoia, and the mightiest of men. Sometimes this idea is overlooked. The divinities within Michelangelo, Leonardo Da Vinci, Alexander Graham Bell, Alexander Solzhenitsyn, and all of the Nobel Peace prizewinners put together, are identical.

Have I opened your eyes? Good.

2

Spiritual Enlightenment

I do want to talk more about the planets and the solar system because, for the longest time, mankind's gaze has been on the ground. Now for those of you who have read my word in my other text, *Into The White Light: The Revelations of Archangel Michael*, I began by saying, "Since creation, mankind has looked upon the heavens," so it may sound like I operate in complete contradiction, but for clarity I absolutely do not. When I spoke about the heavens and when we use that word now, I would like to make the distinction that the word 'heaven' and 'heavens' are reserved for the Kingdom of Heaven.

I would specifically like to offer enlightenment on the fifth dimension, sixth, seventh, eighth and ninth and in doing so, I will quite naturally speak about planets, stars, asteroids, and androids. It is the Aquarian Age. It is also approaching the Herculean Age, and therefore, to better understand these two ages for which you and your children and your children's children will reside in, it is good to know a bit more about them. I say to each of you collectively around the world, look up into the sky, wonder about its mysteries, embrace its complexities, cherish the unknown and do not be afraid of it. Do you know what happens when even a quarter of the people on Earth look up into the sky at the same time? That will be happening in the next ten years—when a quarter of the Earth's population will all be looking up into the sky at the same time. When this happens, it is called an energetic rift. An energetic rift is like a solar flare in its power and its intensity. Before I tell you why so many of you will be looking up into the sky at the same time, I want to assure you that it is not the end of the world. It is not Armageddon. There will be a chain of events, a chain of cosmic events, which will shake three or four galaxies depending upon your view.

Q: Some believe it (2012) represents a very rare cosmological event known as a 'Galactic Alignment.' The fundamental questions therefore are these: Is the galactic alignment capable of effecting Earth in and of itself or is it simply symbolic of a much deeper meaning?

A: I would honor these words, galactic alignment. I am beginning to call light workers in this service, using this term galactic. I am calling light workers and have been in a variety of ways. I suggest to you that the rare cosmological event to which you refer is a result of the Divine Mind. Scientists may differ, so let them. Distant galaxies, galaxies themselves each have Divine Intelligence, Divine Will. It is the same Divine Wisdom that created you and the tiniest of amoebas. To be more specific, the galactic alignment is actually a realignment. Yes, a realignment to the frequencies from another galaxy/galaxies.

Galaxies can be shaken. Ask any scientist and they will tell you this same truth—any galaxy can experience movement, does experience movement, and movement in this instance pertains to shaking. You might be asking yourselves, "Well then Angel, why would three or four galaxies shake in the future?" I say to you, there is an infinitely wise creator who is directing this. Therefore, these three or four galaxies begin to shake and tremble, touch if you will; bump into one another. It may be helpful once again to use your incredible imagination. Imagine bumper cars; each bumper car is a different galaxy and three or four bumper cars collide. (For clarity, the fourth galaxy is not fully formed. That is why I am saying three or four, depending). Remember, galaxies are continually created. When your bumper car has bumped into another one, what happens? There is some sort of sound isn't there? That is exactly what is going to happen slightly after the year 2012. There will be a bumping of these galaxies, a huge around-the-world sound will be heard and everyone's eyes will rise to the skies, looking, searching for what caused this intensely loud and unusual sound. Mothers in Indiana will be calling their children in Texas and asking them if they heard the sound. Fathers in Indonesia will be asking the same of their families, and every one out of four human beings will be doing the same thing, asking the same question, "Did you hear that sound?"

My greatest wish is that you view this as a great discovery, that another galaxy is being born, the fourth one. You might say that it is the loudest global groan of birth ever heard but it is very much a time of birth and of great celebration. So do not fear this when it occurs; embrace it! There will be no earthly damage; no one's eardrums will rupture but the sound globally will be stronger than ten sonic booms, all exploding at the same time. Now, I hear many of you asking about sunspots, solar flares, and other activity around the sun and asking, is this me? Is it another sign of Armageddon as prophesied in the Bible and other texts? I answer, absolutely not. I suggest the Sun is dying and the solar activity will be occurring more frequently, more dramatically. The Sun's influences are her attempts to heal.

When you begin thinking that every living, breathing thing has a consciousness within them, then you will begin to understand that the Sun has a consciousness also. I hope you will view the solar activity, albeit is a bit different from earlier times, as a natural process. You may be asking now, why is the Sun dying? Notice, I say dying, not dead. The Sun will not ever fully die in your lifetime or your children's, children's, children's, children's, children's, children's lifetimes. It is, however, undergoing change in the here and now and certainly in the year 2012. If I were to tell you the Sun has a thin film around the outside of it now, due to mankind's pollutants, would you believe this or would you think it was madness? The solar flares are actually an attempt to burn away this thin film created by mankind throughout time; it is a natural cycle. What do I mean by this? Every time there is an increase in frequency of solar activity, it is in direct relationship to activity emanating from your planet, your world. This time near 2012, it is just like a bigger party. Repeat this—*it is just a natural process of rebirth, regeneration, and restoration.*

Q. Will 2012 bring a lot more violence or any of the other conspiracies (like natural disasters killing everyone?)

A: There is not going to be mass destruction. Lay that fear aside. There is not going to be mass anything…lay that aside. What there will be are shifts. Sometimes, the shifts will create movement. I mean spiritual shift, consciousness shift, energy shift, Mother Earth shift. Nothing will shift to the point of negativity in the ninth degree. Let me try to reassure your minds and hearts that there is God Intelligence, God-Mind, which is greater than anything. Imagine it orchestrating these changes.

As surely as I say this to you now, after this event there will still be souls in the world who view this event as a sign that the world is coming to an end or a sign that Lucifer has taken hold. Neither of these could be further from the truth. Nevertheless, without sufficient wisdom being spread about this event, there are likely to be some pockets of chaos. Do your best right now individually to think in such a way so that only good comes from this. I am asking each of you to take more of a scientific interpretation of these events than you might say a spiritual one, certainly a religious one. Now let's move on to something else. No discussion of planets or galaxies outside of your own would be anywhere nearly complete without a discussion about other life forms. This has been touched upon briefly in this work but it needs to be examined further.

Many of you have seen, perhaps in person, the cave paintings of Lascaux in Southern France, which depict strange shaped beings and strange shaped vehicles. Some of you may have or your mothers or your grandmothers may have seen other like images in their lifetimes. Did you know there is a well in the middle of the African plain, in the middle of the African continent that is completely filled with depictions of what you might call beings not from Earth? I think many of you believe what I am saying here and many of you do not. The beauty of 2012, among the other things previously stated, there will be a global awareness that life in other galaxies does indeed exist and the secretiveness and hidden-ness and yes, even fright of this knowledge will diminish near the year 2012.

In the years following, there will be an increased number in the visibly of recorded and noted encounters with other life forms. With the shift in consciousness with the enlightened thinking coming in with this cosmic shift will be a greater understanding and appreciation for this. There is nothing to fear but fear itself. By and large, the intelligent life forms found on other planets are non-threatening. I say to you in a sense that some of your world leaders should be more fearful for keeping this knowledge from you than anything another life form could demonstrate.

Q: Michael, I am living in America and I think those in politics have not been truthful with us and perhaps to those in other countries as well. What can you teach us about this?

A: It is not my intent to spread fear, only enlightenment. Yes, I would agree that many in power, not just political power, but oftentimes corporation power as well, do not have their soul origin from a galaxy that is pure of light. There are unseen forces, which are at work and continue to be at work, that sabotage the integrity of the human race. This has been going on since the dawning of time. No corner of your globe has been untouched by the alien forces responsible for this. However, let me say this as strongly as I can through this vehicle—THERE IS MORE LOVE AND LIGHT HEALING COMING THROUGH THE UNIVERSE NOW TO RECTIFY AND OVERTHROWN THESE ALIEN INTELLIGENCES THAN AT ANY OTHER TIME IN YOUR HISTORY.

Largely, these other life forms have nothing; send nothing; want nothing, but peace and cooperation. They want harmony, they want acceptance. As souls are firmly in the energy of 2012, by this I mean the second half of 2012, even without consciously doing anything their consciousness will have been raised, shifted. Shifted to what? As stated earlier, greater understanding, greater awareness greater enlightenment because the majority of souls in 2012 will be residing energetically in the fifth dimension, sometimes known as the Age of Aquarius. Therefore, it will be easier for their minds to embrace these ideologies, which I have proclaimed; so let me say this again if you are learning of this before 2012 and simply cannot believe it. Put it down; walk away. Pick it up in 2013 and your view will change.

There will be interstellar colonies as a result of 2012 in the raising of the global vibration. I see the scientists standing and clapping but virtually no one else. By 2012 and the years thereafter, this too, will change. The interstellar communications include travel back and forth within these different dimensions. It may be helpful to think of this time really truly as 'Star Wars' without the war. "Are you trying to say Angel, that in June of 2012 I will be able to take a spaceship, go to another planet, and meet another life form?" To that, I am saying yes. The knowledge to do this already exists. I am saying yes, the *potential* to do this already exists, and I am also saying yes, when this starts to occur, most likely it will be hidden from your view. If I told you that many visitations from other life forms have already occurred, what would you say to this? There are of course the believers and the non-believers. If I went on to tell you that every major world leader has some knowledge of this, would that surprise you? Whenever I speak to souls about other intelligent life forms, I am filled with great promise and hope that mankind will continue to embrace new situations with love, kindness and understanding.

I would like to talk next about two planetary discoveries that I see happening as a result of the enlightened way of thinking being ushered in by 2012. In some way, 2012 can be viewed as the Renaissance; the great Italian Renaissance. Only in 2012, the Renaissance is a global one. There will be more seemingly miraculous discoveries made in the year 2012 through to 2015 than there have been made in your world in the last thirty years and these discoveries will be a direct reflection of the powerful shifting frequencies coming from the other galaxies. What is so encouraging is that many of these wonderful discoveries will be coming from the minds of children. The minds of young Indigo Children are already creating ways for humans to continue to live longer, healthier sustainable lives. Many of the Rainbow Children are already formulating plans for global peace marches. Many Atlantean Children are already working on ways for a New World social order. You have much to be grateful for.

Q: Will we still be having the predicted three days of darkness, and if so, when?

A: Whose prediction, mine? Mankind has lived in spiritual darkness for ages. This will be a time of great celebration and light.

It is very interesting to me that, largely, many questions are fear-driven. Allow me to restate categorically again to erase these fears, there is not going to be an end of the world. ***This is largely an unseen spiritual world battle; the battle of good versus evil, lightness over darkness.*** I would like to expand upon some of the questions honoring each of them from every soul. Let me talk a minute about the questions pertaining to the second coming of Christ. As stated previously, there is going to be a second coming of a Messiah-type figure; but I say to you, he has already arrived. The second coming and the awareness of the second coming will not be globally felt until near the year 2012 but he is in place already. When I say a Messiah-type figure, that is how we are hoping that he will be viewed; not simply as Jesus, a Christian or a Jew, but as a Messiah figure; a Messiah of a more global nature; a Messiah that belongs to all world cultures. Notice, I avoided the word religions. I hear the collective hum of your minds thinking, "Well, where is he, Angel? Where does the new messiah reside then if he is already in our world?" And I say it is not time yet for that to be revealed. Again, I hear the collective hum of doubt asking, "Well why not Angel?" I say to you, there are some divine strategies being used; yes, I like the word strategies.

Q: Will we be required by law to wear the universal code by then? Will people who remain faithful to Jesus be murdered then?

A: I honor all questions but I often wonder how ideas get planted in mankind's consciousness. I know this, yet I do not see. Ask yourselves the question—how do you know what you know? How do you know what you think you know or fear? Is it contained within something you have read? In something you have heard? Where does fear reside? I tell you this mankind! That the shift in consciousness, with the enlightenment there will be no place for fear to rest!

To continue, there are some divine high intelligent strategies in this unseen spiritual battle and one of the strategies is not yet to reveal his placement. However, be assured, in the year 2012 he will be more clearly identified, honored, humbled, noted, and exalted. I would like to make a series of statements that must be made in order for everyone to have an understanding of the complexities of this time in mankind's history. It will also be a time when mankind's life simplifies. There are some dark forces in mankind's world that will need to be abolished and will be abolished. This is not such a revolutionary statement when you think about it spiritually. Since the dawn of time mankind has been defending himself against one enemy or another either the woolly, mammoth or the saber-toothed tiger or the black plague or the church or himself and so on. This statement is not revolutionary, but what is a revelation for some of you is that the darkness that exists in your world originated from another planet. If you still have faith in me, I would like to continue.

What I am trying to say is there are those in your earthly governments whose cell structure came from another dimension. I suppose for some of you it doesn't really matter where evil and greed and corruption come from and to that point, I would agree; but it is what is creating the unseen spiritual battle. Again, 2012 is seen in my realm as the great awakening when mankind's eyes and ears and hearts fully open to the energies of love and kindness. Those who are resistant will battle.

That is why the new Messiah is already in place. Legions of angels are descending upon your world to assist in this cosmic restructuring. If I were to suggest to you that there is a different DNA structure in those souls who possess goodness and those who do not, what would you say? Would you think it might make good dinnertime table conversation? Because this is also true. This ties in beautifully, if you are following my wisdom with the reason for the restructuring of DNA with the Ascension, the fifth dimension Ascension. Most likely, around the world as lightness battles darkness in all of its forms, you will hear of political upheaval. Unless altered, there will be some rioting, looting, and demoralizing behaviors until the overthrow is complete.

This is what World War III will be.

Let me be clear about this. I am not suggesting that men in uniforms will be marching off to war, what I am suggesting is the final bastion, if you will, of good versus evil.

This is the last frontier that needs to be crossed; and it will be crossed by 2015.

Who is making this happen you may be asking yourselves again? Who is making this happen? Is it you, Angel? Is it God? Is it Buddha? Is it Mohammad? Is it Hitler? Is it Stalin? Is it Mother Earth? I say to you, each of you, that there is goodness in this. I answer your questions with a question – where does goodness come from?

Q: "In 2012 will our material world look the same? Will our streets look the same? Will we still drive our cars? Will we still have a government?

A: And I say yes. I say, if you still choose to own a car, you will still drive a car; the sun will still rise in the sky; nightfall will still enter your world, but it will be as if the temperature has changed. By temperature, I mean the feelings associated with living on Earth, again a more enlightened spiritual awareness connecting galaxies and dimensions.

Too many times, in mankind's history, there has been corruption and I am not speaking of corruption purely and solely in the political governing bodies. I will introduce to you the idea of corruption of the land. I will continue to say, throughout mankind's history Mother Earth has been raped, so the universes are reaching out to her; the multi-universes outside of your own are reaching out to her to embrace her with infinite consciousness. I would like to touch on the physical changes that many around the world are feeling within themselves as they begin this Ascension to help you identify some of the symptoms and why they are happening to many of you. As explained earlier, the body is a vessel, your body is a vessel that has been filled with toxins; there are no exception to this. I say even the holiest of holy masters, by laying foot on Mother Earth as she has been polluted; absorbed some level of pollution even if it is in a minute level. Some of you are already beginning to feel the effects of the toxins, or rather the higher energies or higher frequencies entering your world again. It is like a ship that is rocking at sea when a storm is coming; this again is an unseen storm and it is one of golden light. Nevertheless, many of you are like ships rocking in the ocean. Know that this is a temporary situation. Some may be complaining of backaches, pressure in the neck, headaches, fatigue, and nausea and in some cases vomiting and general malaise.

Some of you may be laughing and thinking to yourself, "Angel, this is nothing new. I have experienced these things my entire life," and I say to you, this is exactly the point. These are toxins. This is not how human DNA, not how mankind's health, was created to function! I am attempting to open your awareness and understanding that for those of you who are the most empathetic and most connected to source energetically are going to feel these first and most dramatically. By the time when some of you are reading these words, your symptoms have already passed by a year. My advice during this time, if these are your reactions to the fifth dimensional frequency, is to roll with the punches, to drink a lot of water, read a good book; know this is part of harmonic convergence on the grandest of scales.

As the frequencies are adjusted globally throughout the year 2012, many of you will have many minor symptoms if any at all. Let us examine the years immediately after 2012, because 2012 will be here before you know it like a blink of an eye. I hear the collective world saying to me, "Boy, time is really going fast I don't remember it going so fast before. I can't believe that this and the other happened a year ago." This is all in response to the Earth rotating faster; so the years immediately after 2012 will be seen by us as a plateau of the highest level. The spiritual battle will have been won. The light workers and the divine forces, from whatever galaxy they are from, will continue to work on the molecular DNA structure of any souls who have not yet adjusted energetically. For many, this will be a seamless unseen process. For many grandpas sitting in a chair watching television will be unaware of the happenings. The years 2013, 2014, 2015 will not witness a great change but a great change will have been instilled. What I am trying to say is that even if the soul does not make a conscious effort to be more loving, to be more compassionate, the change will have been made for them.

Q: Will more people become more spiritually aware in 2012 and beyond?

A: In speaking to those who seek answers coming from all different awareness about vibration, energy, the mind, body connection, and frequency, I will try to speak to the most common thread. Yes, as more and lighter workers do their job(s), more and more souls of every description will become spiritually aware. If you are already aware, then your awareness will continue to grow. However, parents please note: Many of your children are already more aware than you! How do you like that?! Yes, children who are more spiritually aware than their elders. What a marvelous concept. Learn from your children. Learn this wisdom. Continue to share the roles of student and teacher.

The young ones, for example, the Indigo Children, are likely to say to their grandpa, "I see purple around you grandpa. I see yellow, I see white, and I see angels." And grandpa will most likely smile with great knowing, not even knowing where the knowing came from, but with a peaceful knowing inside. As a result of living in a higher frequency, many of you will become telepathic, empathic and co-contributors to a new type of nirvana. During the years 2012, 2013, 2014, and 2015 there will be more and more encounters with dimensional beings; less resistance to it, more acceptance to these meetings. Why, because fear will not have a firm foothold. The years 2012 to 2015, mankind will witness incredible expansion in his collective knowledge of the heavens. During these years, many will come to know planets like Herculan, galaxies like the Pleiadian galaxy, interstellar realms like Nebulan and inter-coastal galactic highways.

3

Cosmic Changes

I in continuing our discussion about the integrity of the plant and the animal kingdom, I would like to state this following truth – every time mankind sees an injustice to Mother Earth and the life forms she supports and does nothing about it, you have added a layer of dysfunctionality to oneness. It makes little difference. To go into greater detail about what some of these injustices have been over time. Just imagine though, that if I were to do so, it would take a person about five years to read through the list. Imagine the magnitude of this if this energy were to continue. Therefore, as I stated earlier, cosmic influences, greater dimensional intelligences, are stepping in to help protect Mother Earth and everything she supports. Mankind, humankind gratefully, is rising to the task and by now, I think the task should be clear in your minds. My hope is that it is.

At this point, I would like to focus on some of the proactive ways that mankind will be assisting in the healing of the plant and animal kingdom. As the world nears 2012 and the years beyond, let's examine each hemisphere, because that is how I see it. For those who wish to know a bit more about this, the Northern and Southern Hemispheres show completely distinct energy patterns. I wonder how many of you actually know what the Northern and Southern Hemispheres are comprised of but

I will assume that if you do not, you will be motivated to learn about them. It is my hope that you do. It is my hope, as I speak about the global regions of the world, your home, that everyone becomes more familiar with their home—their global home. What I am asking everyone to do is to look past their windows and expand their interest and knowledge down the street, into the next county, into the next region, and the next hemisphere.

Q: I am in the process of making conditions for the year 2013, but I would be very interested to hear what Archangel Michael as to say about this time.

A: Most assuredly, the cosmic changes, which are already affecting your world, your dimension, your galaxy, though not all galaxies, will extend after 2012. Waves and waves of new knowledge, new discoveries, renewal of plants and animals besides human genome exploration, will be forthcoming. It is Ascension energy. Once given, it cannot be taken away. It has already been given in small doses. Currently, the doses are increasing and will continue to increase until close to 2015 your time, your world.

It is only with appreciation for your entire home that a person truly begins to appreciate the room they are living in. Said another way, this is the time for expanding your thoughts; continuing to open your minds to what is going on in other parts of the world. Let us not lose focus. When I say to expand your hearts to what is going on in other parts of the world, the focus is on what you, one person can do to help determine how Mother Earth will continue to provide a safe and loving home to the plants and animals that dwell within her. In doing this with your thoughts wrapped around the Southern Hemisphere, several things will be occurring in the next decade. The global warming, which many of you are already witnessing, is something that needs immediate attention. This is something that began in the Southern Hemisphere. There is a window of about five years from this moment in time for mankind's thoughts to influence the energy to stop global warming. This I know will be done. Did you know the Aboriginal tribes living in Australia in the year of 2010 have felt the effects of global warming? How do I know this? I see that their food supply has diminished. I see that the polar caps have diminished in size and strength.

However, these are reversible energies if the collective consciousness of the world participates today, and they will. In this regard, I would like to offer the following affirmation – which said globally will affect this consciousness immediately:

"I make a pledge to do what I can to limit my consumption of fossil fuel. I intend to support ways that will nourish Mother Earth and not drain her. I pledge to support interstellar expansion if that is what is necessary to provide Mother Earth the support she needs."

This may mean, if you have a neon sign in your office, no matter where you live in the world, you turn it off and substitute a solar-powered one. If this means you recycle water within your home, then do it. The affects in the Northern Hemisphere of global warming are also being felt and witnessed. Did you know that there are those souls who live in Iceland and Greenland who no longer need the types of clothing they needed before because the temperatures are rising. Now, I have great faith in humankind and I know that with education, with intention, with desire, all things are possible. I hope I am beginning to instill within each of you, desire. Let's examine the Himalayan Mountains and the Andes Mountains, these areas too, have begun to feel the effects of what many are calling global warming. How do I know this? I see the scientists throwing their hands up in the air in disgust, in frustration and sometimes rage, because they cannot get the funding to continue their research in ways in which to reduce ionization, overpopulation, deforestation and so on. Thankfully, this is temporal energy, which will be improving in the year 2012 and beyond. So there's hope.

Did you know at one time there was a yellow-bellied platypus that lived in the outer banks and they lived in proliferation?

Were you aware in Pakistan there was a cobra of gigantic size, which was prolific?

Were you aware that in the Peruvian jungle there was a marvelously genetically unique tsetse fly that was prolific?

In the southwestern United States, were you aware that there was a spiny-toed caterpillar, which held the DNA capability to cure cancer, but it has vanished?

These are just a few of the examples from the animal kingdom that have been removed from your world through mankind's atrocities. The complete list throughout creation, since creation and this point in time, will vary and that is a topic for another time; but let us say that the consensus of creation at the time of creation, numbers roughly fifteen billion.

Pause and reflect upon this.

When souls ask me, "What does the year 2012 mean?" remember, it does not mean simply one thing, just as the word love doesn't mean one thing. It means in part, that there will be an opening for the replenishment of these animal species. That is a huge concept. It means that with the grace of infinite wisdom that divine intervention will be stepping in to facilitate this. So that you too, John, Sarah, Emmanuel, Francesca, Julio, Sebastian, Ping, will have an opportunity to become involved. How wonderful this news is, knowing that your thoughts, your actions, along with the divine wisdom, are going to replenish your world. Some of the things you can expect to see will be the discovery of new species. Let us begin with the animal species. I should say, I suppose, a rediscovery. Because what is going to happen is that scientists are going to rediscover many of the species that were wiped out. What I am saying is the restoration, the rejuvenation, the restructuring of the global energy at this particular time in your history is allowing this to happen.

In addition, there will be new forms of plant and animal life – brand new, brand, brand new, being discovered in the next ten years. And like the souls who have entered in with restructured DNA, these new forms of plant and animal life will also have newly restructured DNA. This means the new plants and animals, which will be discovered in all parts of the world, will have a conscious intelligence that matches the conscious intelligence of the Crystalline Children; the Rainbow Children; the Aquarian Children. What does this mean? It means that many of the newly found plants and animals will be able to function at a higher level. What does that mean you ask still?

It means, for example, that it will be easier for these new plant and animal species to reproduce; they may be seen as biotic. I would suppose in some ways you could call them biotic, some will call them biotic; it doesn't really matter what you call them; it simply means that Mother Earth is healing. When these new plant and animal farms are discovered, many of them will hold the keys to the healing of mankind's illnesses. Many of them will hold the keys to spinal regeneration, cloning of themselves, so when there is a bare spot within the land, one new species of tree will procreate so quickly and easily it will fill the land.

This type of synchronicity between the plant and animal kingdom is something being orchestrated and known in my realm as harmonic convergence. What it means to you is that it is as individualized as your thumbprint. It is a very magnificent and blessed event. Sometime, a long time ago, the DNA blueprint for your planet became lost. Maybe, even, you might say, was abducted. With 2012, and the decade following, the abduction will have been completely abolished. So if I have spoken to you already privately, let me say this ties in perfectly to my use of the words "a new world order." Depending upon where you live and what you prescribe to, you may have heard these words "new world order" from multiple sources. What I have just described as the *new world order*, it is the time of the great spiritual awakening, the time of the great consciousness shift.

Returning to our previous discussion about landmass and water mass for a moment. With the new species of plants, that will be entering in and have already started to enter your world, there are going to be some seismic shifts in the Earth to allow these higher frequency plants to take root. It is my hope and desire that every soul be protected from harm when these seismic shifts will occur. Once these new plant species, these new biotic are rooted in a frequency of seismic eruption, the seismic shifts will diminish greatly. Much of this, as you are reading these words, has already occurred. The same holds true for the integration of the animal world within the great oceans. There will be some activity in both of your hemispheres as the global waters adjust to the higher frequencies. These are temporary, and for the most part, are already subsiding. Within each of these new plant and animal species will be a nugget of molecular encoding that will ensure mankind's sustainability for eons and eons of time. If you can think about this as each new species having a little secret note within them, a very positive secret note, then you will approach understanding of what it is I see. No one in the world, no place in the world, will not receive this wisdom. Every continent, every country, both hemispheres of the oceanic plane will be receiving some form of new life. How great 2012 is!

Q: Can you discuss the significance of the Venus Transit of 06-06-12 (eight Earth years = thirteen Venus years almost exactly. The transit gives Venus and Earth five perfect kisses, a cycle making a perfect pentagram. 5,8,13 belong to the Fibonacci sequence — defining phi.)

A: How many times am I asked this! More and more, yes, this is good and wise thinking as all thinking is good and wise. Whenever Venus turns direction, Venus creates a marvelous opportunity for love expansion. You mention the word kiss and that is exactly the word vibration associated with each planet. Did you know that each planet has an earthly vibration associated with it? True. Perhaps some of you will wish to engage your mind further. With Venus having the word vibration of love expansion which is exactly what is happening now, this brings me to another pausing point—and that is to allow each of you to try to identify other major turns of Venus when in your world or world's history love expanded.

Jump forward in time and go to the year 2015, because sometimes learning about new concepts is made easier by comparison; in about the year 2015, there will be another wave of harmonic convergence. Harmonic convergence is an interstellar inter-dimensional set of frequencies likened to the new set of frequencies entering your world and accumulating in the year 2012. This too, is great news, you may think of 2012 as round one. In about and near the year 2015, there will be an explosion of interstellar communication/interstellar travel. There is nothing to be fearful of; I am purposefully introducing this to your ears now so that you are not fearful of this.

Many other universes exist outside of the one you know. Near and about 2015 more and more global awareness will be centered around this idea more; evidence will be seen and experienced. It is necessary for the future development for all future generations. If I told you that by the year 2015 half of the souls living in your world today will be calibrated to the fifth dimension where I often reside, how would that make you feel? This is the truth.

To restate, the fifth dimension is in sharp contrast with the present world dimension; being the fourth, it is a vibration of total love and kindness. Imagine that half of the world's population will energetically be residing in the fifth dimension. Now, it is time for me to jump up and down again. Before the year 2020, three-quarters of the world's population will be residing in the fifth dimension and by 2030 the rest. Now I am really jumping up and down. Is the promise; this is the truth.

You may be asking yourselves then, "I'll be on the Angelic Realm then?"

And this I say to you with total love and gratitude, yes, you will be. We have been waiting.

By 2015, another generation of helper souls, helper children, children with higher vibrations than your own, will be introduced. They will be known by several names and perhaps received by no name at all. But understand and find comfort that this process of energetic oneness, this shift in spiritual consciousness toward oneness, is in a sense ongoing. What a beautiful thing, knowing that the higher frequencies of 2012 are going to keep coming and coming and coming. There will be a time in the not so distant future when many in your world will proclaim their world as nirvana.

How will you recognize these children in your timeframe I have just stated? They will most likely be your children's children. To interject some humor, I will say they may be thought of as the Cadillacs of Cadillacs; with their arrival will come the second coming of the master known as Jesus Christ.

There are a few more points to consider before leaving the wisdom of 2012 and beyond; item one; there are many in the political arenas around the world who will be overthrown; either spiritually or realistically, for the truth that they carry simply does not resonate truth any longer. When this occurs in your part of your world, this should be seen as another way in which Mother Earth is healing. I am not asking you to demonstrate, incite or participate in riots, invite anger or any other negative emotion when this occurs; I am asking each of you to humbly, gracefully, gently, embrace the realization that these changes are necessary and will promote healing. I am asking for your patience and cooperation as these events are settled into place. Please do not use words like chaos or shambles in your discussion with others; when these changes start occurring they are simply to be seen as a shift. Think of them more as shifting sands, and you personally will be in a better place and each of you collectively will be taking an active role in healing your home. Do not allow fear to become a part of your vocabulary, in many cases as stated already, fear is a vibration which won't be able to take hold; it won't be able to take up residency.

I would like to speak for a moment about the air because Mother Earth cannot heal, you cannot live, plants and animals cannot flourish, without pure clean air. Air has a consciousness just as everything else has a consciousness. Right now, I am speaking of earthly air. Ask any scientist you know, and she will tell you that there are different air qualities in different galaxies. In honoring the air you breathe, I am taking this moment to educate and proclaim that the air that nourishes you and sustains you will be elevated in consciousness in 2012. If I told you that, your air, in your world, in your galaxy actually appears yellow or yellow tinged to me, do you think this is a good thing or a not so good thing? Well, I will tell you currently it can be viewed as a not so good thing. The closer you get to 2012 however, the purer the air will become. It will appear to me again as pureness appears to me, as crystal clear. Crystal as it pertains to crystalline energy.

Q: Are the changes already happening? I believe there is no need to live in fear, that the changes will be all good, like totally different government policies and leaders, the money market will crash so we will all trade with each other, basically total social restructuring will allow a more caring and loving human race to move into higher vibrational dimension. The GOLDEN AGE that we have waited over 2000 years for is happening NOW. If we embrace it, we will all be fine. Is this correct, Angel?

A: I suggest to you that it is an age over two thousand years in the creation, or rather, re-creation. Changes within the social systems will occur but crash and collapse are words that I do not honor. Instead, I will say that humankind is going to keep experiencing a revolution. What kind of revolution—a spiritual one of cosmic proportions. Keep loving, keep embracing.

4

The Rising of Atlantis

Let us now discuss the lost city of Atlantis.

Because earlier in the text we have talked a little bit about Atlantean children without going into much explanation of what Atlantean Children and the resurfacing of Atlantis has to do with energies of 2012. The lost city of Atlantis is a city that will be renewed in the decade to come. This is a city and a civilization. Moreover, it was a vibrational frequency put into an emotion by intelligent life forces from another dimension. The lost city of Atlantis is located in the Great Barrier Reef, off Australia's East Coast. What I suggest to your mind is that the lost city of Atlantis will be given rise again in the decade to come, I mean this very literally in the sense that the life energies that exist above the ground can also co-exist underground or in the water as in this case. Let me say this again, that as human beings the thoughts you create, the lives you have been living, the communities, and the consciousness in which you know, are also being paralleled under the water. Finally, said another way, your world consciousness is shifting, is also shifting under the great oceans of your world. There are magnificent tunnels that have been created by intelligent life forces that have yet to be discovered. They will be discovered in the next decade. If your mind can imagine space colonies then I trust that your magnificent minds can imagine oceanographic colonies, systems of civilization if you will.

If I went on to tell you the pyramids in Egypt, particularly those found in Giza, the Giza Plateau, are markers for an opening directly underground for one of these underground water tunnels, would your mind be able to accept this as truth? The area of Giza is not the only area in your global world that is seen by us in my realm as a marker for these underground tunnels. As you try to understand what I am communicating, the tunnels are representations for civilizations. They are not merely tunnels as tunnels are. Clearly, many of you know that your world was once completely covered in water. It is to these consciousnesses, which I am speaking.

The lost civilization of Atlantis will be recognized as a global discovery of mind-blowing proportions. Who and how will the continent be discovered? As incredulous as this may sound, in the next ten years as a result of the great shift of spiritual consciousness, there is going to be a huge tidal wave, which rises up out of the ocean of the Great Barrier Reef exposing the lost civilization. For many people living fear-based lives, your minds have already leapt to the conclusion that this will be a horrific tragedy with thousands of lives lost. For those more trusting and awakened, it will be merely seen as an extension of the 'New World Order.' If any of you who have seen those cartoons in any language, where heroic feats are performed by those of super strength, this is sort of how you can image the event that I am trying to describe. That is an opening up of one of the largest oceanographic tectonic plates in the Southern Hemisphere to expose an advanced civilization. Since this is tied into the Earth's development and transformation, this should be viewed as another time of great celebration. It may take fifteen years for everyone or for the majority of souls on Earth to become aware of this event; for there will be those in power who will try to hide it, just as they have hidden many things from mankind's eyes for centuries.

With the awakening, many untruths will be exposed. If I told you that many governments are already aware of underwater colonization and are hiding it from mankind, what would you say? This is divine truth. If I went on to repeat that many foreign governments continue to hide information about higher intelligent life forms, would this also surprise you? 2012 and the decade beyond will be a time when fear will not have a place to hang its hat. Lies and corruption will not have a leg to stand upon. The further you get into the decade after 2012 the more frequent and prolific this information will be revealed to me, this is a very good and wise thing. Truth always will resonate at the highest vibration.

Repeating, the City of Atlantis will be rising again. Your collective minds may wonder, 'Why is this happening? Why should I care; how will this affect me? How will this affect my children and my children's children? I am afraid.' I say to each and every one of you who may be thinking these thoughts, to breathe release and affirm; *"I am in the holiest of places with my thinking. I know that my world is kind and loving. I trust what the Angel has prophesized will better my world in some way."*

Just as there has been an unseen spiritual battle since before your world was created, there have also been unseen battles amidst the ocean floor. The rising or the resurrection of the city of Atlantis will signify an end to this battle; love and kindness will be victorious. I mentioned one marker being the area of Giza; I would like to mention some others for your understanding. Before I go on to do that, let me add that for most of you, the information just shared about the City of Atlantis, the lost civilization of Atlantis, will merely be a curiosity. Another marker to the oceanographic world is in Eastern Pakistan. There is also a marker in South Western Brazil and a marker in Bogotá, Columbia. There is also a marker near Beijing, China and one near the Province of Alberta, Canada. These were the major portal points when higher intelligence came to your dimension to develop the underground civilizations, which are the tangible evidence of consciousness. Therefore, when I say they established civilizations, they were establishing higher vibrational consciousnesses.

There is great unity in the divinity of this wisdom between the galaxies and the cosmos. So if twenty years from now you run across some information a new continent has been discovered, do not say I didn't tell you so. This discussion naturally leads into a bit more detailed exposé or examination of higher life forms. 2012 and the immediate years following thereafter more and more information will be revealed about the other intelligent life forms in other galaxies. For those who wish to learn a bit more about this, I will say there are some nefarious inter-dimensional life forms that will continue to try to play havoc with your world's transition from the fourth dimension to the fifth. These efforts will be largely unsuccessful.

Q: Professor Stephen Hawking, a theoretical physicist from Great Britain, contests Sir Isaac Newton's belief that the universe must have been designed by God. He believes that the universe can and will create itself from nothing. He wrote that is why the universe exists, why we exist. What is your divine wisdom in this as it relates to creation?

A: I honor all wisdom from your world. It has come to my attention, that some like Professor Hawking have this thought…that the universe is totally and fully capable of creating itself. I will acknowledge wisdom within this concept. Perhaps my interpretation of the 'Big Bang' Theory will shed some light on the concept. I say to each of you without hesitation or delay that your world and all of the planets in the solar system and solar systems have an intelligence, a Divine Intelligence. What does Mr. Hawking think enables him to think these thoughts? His liver? I mean this in all seriousness. I invite challenged thinking. It is every bit as important in evolution—challenged thinking—as the Darwinian theory of evolution. Do planets, galaxies and alternate planes of reality have the ability to create oneself? Yes, of course. Was there an intelligent force that brought RISE THE need for the universe TO create? Yes. This is where this soul made, to my thinking, a misstep of analytical thinking. It is more important I feel when talking and educating about creation, the cosmos, the Infinite Wisdom in all things that we look at the diversity in creation, not further divide humanity into arguing, fighting, quarreling over this concept. As long as there has been oxygen to breathe, there has been an intelligence that created oxygen to breathe in your world, hydrogen in other worlds, and a combination of hydromagnetic fields, which can support life.

I suppose it could be said that the real aspect of this discussion is who is God?

So I will say to you, ask yourselves, who is God? Is it yourself? Is there not God in every plant, and living thing from the single celled nuclei to the omnipotence of all thirty-six and more dimensions of which I am aware? Is it dharma? Is it Kundalini? Is it Sumatric Philosophy? It God a man? A woman? Omnipotent? What about Mother Earth; is she not God? This is where clarity can be imparted more universally. So I will take this opportunity to teach and say that it makes no difference to those of us in this fifth dimension what each of you believes to be God, or how you define God/Infinite Mind/Mother Earth, Shiva/ Krishna, the stars, your spark. What is more important to your soul growth is that you honor something. That you honor all that is living, including the infinite universes, both parallel and curvilinear.

Those souls who have had implants and attachments will be freed from them. Implants will also be impossible to affect future generations forever more since their DNA has been altered. This should be seen as other news for great celebration. ImI I plants for those unfamiliar are usually not always genetic codes to alter a human's DNA or more simply you might say, soul.

Many of you are already aware, throughout time your world has been visited by space ships, spacecraft, and unidentified flying objects. Sometimes, during these encounters, the visits were from nefarious beings with the intention of sabotaging your Earth's development by taking human specimens against their will and implanting them with altered strands of DNA. With the arrival of 2012, this will no longer be possible. Praise GOD and the Infinite Mind!

I will pause here for your reflection.

Allow me to state that my intent here is not to confuse anyone but to offer love, clarity and hope. I can hear many blaspheming me already, questioning my sanity, my divinity. In some minds, I have stated that to their way of thinking, "How can there be a GOD if this goes on?" So I say to those of you who may be blaspheming me right now that my love goes out to you tenfold. That I say to you that God is man and woman combined, the God mind, the Infinite Mind Intelligence which created multi-realities and multi-dimensions did so unaided. My intent in this text is not to become a theologian and defend theology, but rather open up hearts and minds to greater things to come. It is such a blessing that very soon negative implants will no longer be able to take hold. This can be seen as another thread of what is meant by the reality of 2012.

Do you know how many souls throughout mankind's history have suffered from the effects from an otherworldly implant? The number would stagger you. When a soul has been implanted, they cannot live lives filled with peace and happiness, joy and laughter. How great this news is to think that thousands and thousands of souls who have been denied this ability will once again obtain it.

We were not finished with our discussion of Atlantis and it has also been brought to my attention that many souls are asking for guidance about the Sirians. Therefore, I will be happy to continue speaking of Atlantis and introducing knowledge of the Sirians. The lost continent of Atlantis to continue is going to be heralding a new dawn and the new dawn is as stated previously, an elixir of life. It is however not the only discovered ancient wisdom that will be known to your world in the years ahead. Those energies that are responsible for the rising of Atlantis will also be responsible for the rising of other lost civilizations such as the Incan, the Mayan, the Egyptian, the Roman, the Ottoman or Turkish.

You may be asking yourselves, "Well, there are other lost empires Angel, why don't you mention these?" and I say to you, perhaps one day

I will, but for now as it is structured the best parts of these civilizations, these empires will be coming to the surface of human awareness. Notice, I said the *best parts*; this is where you might say that the Mayan prophecies tie in as a thread. The truth, which has been written, is that, the Mayan calendar prophesied this reawakening, to which I will agree. Across the world from The Great Barrier Reef and the lost continent of Atlantis, which will be, renamed Sirius, it is where the new Mayan energy will emerge. I am not suggesting that another landmass will be forming itself in the next one hundred years but, I am suggesting that there is a special set of energetic frequencies which are already in place for this to be. So that in the next two hundred to three hundred years there will be a newly discovered landmass again rising from the floors of the ocean off the coast of Mexico near Costa Rica.

If you can imagine the energies of a high intelligence floating over this area of the world and you have x-ray vision like some say I do, and some of you do, then this is what you can image what I am talking about. And this energy is filled with love, kindness, acceptance, non-judgment, peace and harmony. In fact, all of the other energetic markers that I will be describing, which is the lost continent previously mentioned, will have these same characteristics. Shifting now to the essence of the Roman Empire…the word essence means the very best eternal sense of something. *Es-sence* – look it up; become familiar with the word *essence* if you desire. For example, the essence of the gardenia is the beautiful aroma; the essence of the sun is its healing warmth. So the essence of the Roman Empire is being birthed now. And it is being birthed over the landmasses of present day Italy, Sicily, and Croatia. For your understanding, the same energy essence of the Egyptian empire is already forming over the present day Sahara desert. When these three energies surface on Earth, most likely most of you will be seeing this from the Kingdom of Heaven. The essence of the Incan Empire will be found in the Amazonian basin.

What this means though, however, and why I feel it is useful about this energy forming now, is to fill you with wisdom, spiritual truth, hope and enlightenment. We in the divine realm like to work like this; we like to facilitate cosmic multi-universal changes in many dimensions not just yours and we do this in other dimensions and your dimension Earth by working in what some call, and I will call for now, quadrants. So that the quadrants in which I am trying to identify; the first round primary quadrants of Ascension, will be the Mayan Empire, the Roman Empire, the Egyptian Empire, Incan Empire and the Atlantean Empire.

This same approach to consciousness raising, if you will, has been done in other galaxies as well. It is much easier to lift up an object if you lift up by all four corners than if you try to hook it up from the middle. Imagine, if you will for a moment, that within each of these renewed civilizations, the best part of their contributions are given a new life. Imagine what this means; I will guide you. I suggest that one of the Roman essences from the mighty Roman Empire in your world was actually the essence of courage. I am not saying that mankind interpreted the essence of courage properly but I am saying from a spiritual standpoint that was the soul essence of that particular empire. And yes, particular empires can have soul essences just as an individual can.

I suggest to you that the essence of the Incan civilization/empire was telepathy. Again, not the entire empire's history demonstrated the highest essence of telepathy and communion, but nevertheless that is the essence; the highest, the purest form of telecommunicating between heaven and Earth, was the essence of the great Incan civilization and it is the energy, which is building there again now and will be built upon in the decades to come. For your understanding, would any of you like to guess what the essence of the Mayan culture the Great Mayan Empire was? No, it wasn't barbarism. No, it wasn't persecution. It was faith. I hear some of you having dissension with this idea and while I honor this, if you are following me on this, what I am trying to communication is that mankind before mankind's actions, mankind's thoughts did not fulfill the soul essence of any of these empires, but the promise is that this next time mankind will. The soul essence of the Egyptian Empire, would anyone want to take a guess? It is resourcefulness. Lastly, the soul essence of the lost continent of Atlantis is harmony. Later, there will be a second round of other civilizations, which come to be reborn again, not to discount any soul that may have ancestors or be themselves from another region not mentioned. Do not confuse your worth with what I am talking about here neither exalt it nor diminish it. Rather, understand that the globalness of what will be affecting future generations.

The level of potential for loving one another will be at its highest peak since the dawn of creation. You might imagine it this way; that in the next several decades your entire world will be seen as one great Italian renaissance with every soul producing great beauty in thought, action and deed.

Sirius

As mentioned, the lost continent of Atlantis will be renamed Sirius or shall we say *be* named Sirius because it will be a new realization in a sense not to be confused with Syria or Damascus. But Sirius as in the eighth dimension; Sirius as in another dimension outside of your own; Sirius as in a collective intelligence outside of your own; Sirius as a set of stars or a constellation already known by many. It is indeed the Sirian people or the Sirian race if you will, who will assist in giving rise to this particular energy. Some of you may already be familiar with the Sirians or the Sirian energy; they are very different from the Pleiadians and the Pleiadian energy because, simply put, they originated from another dimension. To make the mistake that they are one in the same would be a bit like comparing apples to oranges. Some of you may even remember King Sirius from your studies. If you do, then I congratulate you. If you haven't, do not internalize this because the important concept in sharing this with you is to restate differently that there are many dimensional beings from many dimensions, which your world will be learning of in 2012 and in the years beyond. Plato, the astronomer knew this, knew of them. Leonardo da Vinci, the great thinker and mathematician, knew of them, believed in this concept. Many great masters/thinkers of Eastern Indian traditions also have known of this. The difference is, however, that more of mankind will come to accept this as truth. Why? For one thing, there will be more and more sightings of extraterrestrial beings after the arrival of 2012 and secondly, the ability for those in power to cover these visitations up will be diminished. If your mind can leap into two hundred years from now, imagine ten different colonies being developed from higher life forms; from other dimensions; as this is how it will be.

I would like to shift gears a bit back to a more comprehensive discussion about good versus evil during this period and lightness overcoming darkness; because this can be seen as a thread of 2012; lightness overcoming darkness. Some in your world are asking "Does 2012 mean there will be a second coming of Christ?" and I say to you, yes, in some sense that 2012 will signify the time there will be a dramatic rise in Christ consciousness but Christ is not the only holy master. All holy masters who have lived in your world have been anointed to return. It is within each of you, that is where the new awareness should lie—within you.

Allow me to restate this again, because this is very important and cause for great celebration. The years of 2012 and beyond will see the resurrection of the soul essence all of the masters that have walked your Earth. How great and glorious a divine plan is this! New holy masters offering new and even more profound wisdom and healing will be born. Three new masters will be born amongst the ones your world already knows. The other major distinction in this wisdom is that the masters will not represent earthly religion any longer. The masters will be seen as spiritual masters; they will no longer have a chain or a link attached to a particular sect. Halleluiah! Shalom! Namaste! Now, if you are imagining this future, you are imagining your world with new eyes; you're also imagining your world as you yourselves are raised in consciousness.

Your entire planet is evolving to the point so that everyone on it is a master, a spiritual master. During this process, there are going to be some interruptions in the flow; darkness you might say, because at any time, in any galaxy when the power of Ascension increases so does the attempt of darkness to increase. The key word to focus on here is *attempt*. Thinking of it this way—if you are outside on a sunny day and you could lift yourself off in a backpack rocket propelling device so you could approach the sun, the closer you got to the sun, the more blinding the light would be. If you are in the white light, you wear sunglasses, simply reach into your pocket, and put them on. If you are not in the white light, the white light blinds you. You are frightened. It might even cause you some pain. So, while the global Ascension process is going on, there will be uprisings of a dark nature, most of these will be unseen. As I say, though my words seem real, I am a spiritual being in a spiritual dimension or dimensions; so largely this statement relates to unseen spiritual battles of goodness versus evil.

Some have come to me to ask, "I have heard that the devil is coming again to Earth in 2012 as well, Angel?" To which I say, this is impossible. Are there dark unseen forces at work in your world today? Yes, absolutely so. Are these dark forces the devil; absolutely not, for there is no such thing as the devil. There are soul particles that will be forever grey without change without light, goodness, and salvation. Expect an evil one to rise out of the lands of South Africa; expect an evil one to rise out of the United Kingdom; expect an evil one to rise out of the United States of America. It is likely their energy will give rise to uprisings. We in the angelic realm are battling this every day and we are winning; you who are spreading light and goodness are battling this also every day of your lives. Light will be victorious by 2012.

This concludes part one.

5

Other Life Forms/Time Travel

Much has already been written about other intelligent life forms but only it has been covered up. You might call this the discoveries if you wish because one of the discoveries is the hiding of the Reptilian race. Let me say this another way, in this period we are talking about attempts from those in power all over the world in every major continent have been made to cover up the existence of many truths, the existence of Reptilians is merely one example. So my intent in this is not to frighten anyone but to take the conjecture out of the equation by clearly describing what Reptilians are, what they mean to do, what you can expect from them and what has been done to hide their presence. By and large, there are a few examples of which I am a literal guide. Reptilians reside in a light galaxy thirteen hundred Earth soul light years away from yours and they exist for one reason and one reason only—to keep the energy of your world—your Earth from ascending. Now I have said the worst of the worst.

Reptilians

They walk on two legs. Unlike your skin, they have scaly skin. They have eyes but unlike your two eyes, their two eyes can see in the dark and their two eyes are translucent. Their skin color is from light grey to a greenish brown. They range in height from 5'7" to roughly 7' in height. They have ear openings, but no ears such as yours. Unlike mankind, they have like a tail that can vary from a very short one to a longer one that drags to the ground. Needless to say, they are not something to gaze upon in admiration. Their faces do not resemble Botticelli's 'Birth of Venus' or any other sea nymph for that matter. Unlike the human form, they are heartless, have one lung, a digestive system that is completely different from yours and no sense of smell. What they do have, you might say, is hard wiring that is totally telepathic and demonic in nature.

We have been fighting them off since before your world came into creation. I have no fear of them and neither should you. They pose no threat unless you allow the threat. If I said that Adolph Hitler was a Reptilian, what would you say? A few of you may have an instantaneous knowingness, a few more of you may think that it could be true but most likely the majority of souls will say that I am foolish. However, the majority of souls would agree that this particular soul possessed energies, negative energies that were out of this world. Hitler is one obvious dramatic example of a soul who was attached with Reptilian energy. Generally, this has been hidden from mankind's awareness but one day it will be discovered and fully revealed. If I enlightened you to the fact that there was a book secretly kept by those in high order that listed all of those souls, those evil souls that had been identified as Reptilians, you may be astounded. But nevertheless, it is the truth. The whereabouts of the book remains a mystery, as it is in constant motion from place-to-place from guard-to-guard to prevent discovery.

Nevertheless, one day in the nearest future, the book and the wisdom in it will be discovered. Here are some names for your understating of other earthly souls that contained or were attached to Reptilian energy and in no particular order they are Genghis Khan, Sigmund Freud, Noriyoshi Ishishema, Charles de Gaulle and thousands of others. It can go without saying that there is no need to name these souls, for my intention here is not to spread mistrust or anxiety or bitterness on any level only to give example that largely the Reptilians chose to affect or infiltrate those in positions of high power or become those in high power themselves. Depending on the level of infiltration by a Reptilian, a soul from Earth might have low levels of deception, treachery, hatred, bigotry and violence within them or any degrees of the highest amounts. I trust that I am making some sense.

I wish to say that throughout mankind's history there are those in political power who have learned the existence of those in which I am speaking in ways that have even shocked themselves. Discovery of truth, no matter what the truth, is always wise and holy. Just as I described underground tunnels in the ocean where much good colony building is going on, there are also tunnels dug into mother Earth that the Reptilians have drilled to burrow and leech off mankind's energy, power and joy. If you can imagine a leech, then you have imagined the essence of the Reptilians. They will however, be exposed and once and for all, implode.

Discovery number two: many all over the world resent those in power. This is nothing new or Earth shattering. It will come to be a widely upheld belief that many in places of power are simply corrupt; again this is nothing new. The pharaohs in Egypt were often corrupt, corrupt Chinese landlords, corrupt Bulgarian taxmen, corrupt Finnish dockworkers and so on. But the reason for their corruption will be seen as something coming from another dimension or another world; this is what the new discovery will be about, not that a corruption exists but from where this corruption originated. A flower cannot grow in a garden full of weeds. With the Ascension energy, the weeds will be trampled down by the footprints of love. What a marvelous experience to come. As long as I am speaking of discoveries, many new and wonderful discoveries will also fall into mankind's awareness. As this Ascension energy takes hold, fewer and fewer diseases of the body will be manifested for mankind all around the world. There will be no more AIDS, no more cancers, no more heart disease, and very few premature deaths. It will be the rise in your consciousness and your children's consciousnesses, which will allow this to be.

I say to you do not worry, argue, condemn or swear over healthcare reform. For in the short future there will be no need for healthcare of any kind. Cells have memory; cells can change memory. Said another way, the Ascension energy, the shift in consciousness, is allowing cells to change their memory from one of deception, distrust, and disease to health. It's that simple. Of course, healing oneself is not a new idea; it has been done every day and has been done for thousands of years but what is new, what will be new is that enough people in quantity now will be aware that their thoughts create wellness that they will wipe out diseases of a global nature.

I would like to restate, look for no more cancer because there will be none. Look for no more AIDS, for there will not be any. Look no more for health disease as there will be none. Look for no more premature death and aging for there will not be any.

Space Colonies

Satellite information continues to assist us in relaying much positive information from the cosmos to your world. I would ask each and every one of you to become more aware of the connection between space and Earth. I have yet to talk very little about outer space colonies. I would like to talk about that next in detail as this too, can fall under the heading of discoveries of 2012 and beyond.

Galaxies are continually being created each and every second of each and every day. You may not know of them but they are. Some die off and don't last, and others grow in size and influence until they are recognized. Because your world is spinning at a faster velocity now than in any other time in mankind's history, the ability or ease for these colonies to develop will be intensified. It is likely and hopeful that your children and your children's children will be commuting to distant galaxies, new colonies. This will be so. The colonies will be created through the higher intelligence, which is being absorbed by those in your world already; those who have ascended to a place with little fear or no fear will make the first journeys.

The colonies might be seen as satellite space stations but I prefer to call them colonies because they will be more like colonies in the sense that they are environments, and less like robots. This will be true for all over your world understanding again that when the divine mind creates in tandem; light, dark, man, woman, left, right, yin, yang, colony on the right hemisphere, colony on the left. I am asking each of you to remove from your thinking that only the Chinese will have space colonies because only the Chinese are enlightened enough for this. This is simply untruth. Space colonies will be popping up like flowers in the global garden. "For what purpose?" you may be asking. For the purpose to continue spreading light and love to other galaxies; I have already taught that there is more than one galaxy; so it will be desire to do this, not a *have to*, but a *want to* create these colonies. This is not five hundred years into the future truth. Will these colonies be built tomorrow, probably not. I said *probably*. Will they be built in the next one hundred years? Most likely so. The space between the galaxies will diminish. Why is this so? One answer: for oneness, for complete oneness.

It is not because Mother Earth will be running out of resources; it is not because there will be so many people on your planet that they will need another place to live. It will not, for either of those reasons or any of a dozen others that I have heard. It is so the soul can experience oneness. Now this needs clarification – can oneness be achieved on Earth? Yes, absolutely certainly. But the oneness I am speaking about here has to do with the Infinite Mind that created all of the galaxies that are created now and will be created in the future. That is the oneness to which I speak. Give your mind some time to reflect upon this.

Grays

First of all, I want to make it clear for your understanding that Grays are not to be feared. When I say the word *Gray*, I am talking about other forms of life outside of your own. The reasoning behind our continued discussion of other life forms is simply to dispel fear because more and more information will be uncovered in the upcoming years about the truth of their existence. More and more sightings will be written about, spoken about, and telegraphed in your world. Some of you may find it fascinating that Grays have been visiting your planet before mankind inhabited it. Throughout your earthly time, Grays have been found in all parts of the world. Generally, their appearance is as follows; they tend to be smaller than Reptilians and generally less menacing looking, many have extremely large friendly eyes. Their skin, for the most part, is soft like yours, although they refer to their skin as their outer layer.

There are many categories of Grays and subcategories of Grays. It is not my intent to speak of every subcategory; but to place the idea in your mind about the abundance and infinite creative forces that give rise to many different forms of intelligences. Grays visit your world any time they are called upon or anytime they feel there is a need. They are to be viewed as benevolent. They have a consciousness or a frequency that emits a resonance of compassion. Their intent and their purpose is to help your world, the Earth, evolve.

Thousands of individuals have actually already seen Grays. Thousands more have imagined them and have called them Martians. They are neither Martians nor aliens. The word *alien* should only be used when referring to the Reptilians, for their purpose is alien to that of mankind's. Native Americans have long known of the importance of the Grays in their spiritual teachings and cultural ceremonies. High in the hills of the Peruvian Andes is a sacred spot that the Grays call home. Many have seen the Grays in this sacred spot. Images of Grays have been recorded in stone and mortar in cave dwellings all over the world.

If you have ever wondered what their space ship might look like when they visit the Earth, I will tell you that the ship tends to be appearing more like an oval disc than a high-rise with legs. Other intelligent forms of life use this structure. I am aware of at least five other intelligent life forms in the multi-galaxies, perhaps there are more, perhaps more will be created. All things are possible within the God Mind. I would like to restate that they are benevolent and offer no harm.

Androids

I'd like to continue this examination by discussing Androids. Android is not a satellite. The *Android* I am speaking of does not have wings. Android is a general term; a broad-based term describing any complex relationship between man and other beings. Androids are responsible for the development of many advanced technologies and many super-evolved theories, some of which have affected your world's development. If you can imagine an Android as a giant robotic mind, this would be fairly accurate. I am not suggesting that Androids reign supreme over all dimensions and all galaxies. I am not stating in any way they compete with God and the God Mind. In some ways, they can be seen as the interstellar managers running systems, keeping currents flowing and offering multilateral communication between all platforms. The use of the word *platforms* here means consciousness.

Near the year 2014, there will be new earthly discoveries about the existence of Androids. My intent is not to create fear but to lessen any that may be forming and to demonstrate the forms of creation are limitless. A long time ago in a far distant galaxy about three hundred million light years from yours, something of a huge magnetic proportion occurred. The occurrence was the splitting of the atom. For those physicists who may be reading these words, I will say to them that the splitting of the atom created the different galaxies. This will fall upon their ears as softly as a gentle rain; for others, this wisdom may feel like a hailstorm.

Q: I have heard of the Annunakis and the Twelfth Planet. Who were they and what do they want from us?

A: The Annunakis are nefarious entities or beings from the Twelfth Planet sometimes called the Red Planet. Where is the Red Planet? It is located five thousand light years outside of the Sun's solar system. Before man was living on Earth, there were global tribesmen in space if you can imagine. Most of the global tribesmen were in existence to bring higher intelligence to Earth and other forming planets such as Mercury and Mars. Most of the global tribesmen or higher intelligent life forms did their job wonderfully and completely and their job was to go to Earth and help stabilize a society, which would be founded upon love and freedom. The Pleiadians were one group of the tribesmen who did their job well. Others from the Star Nation have done their job well also.

Unfortunately, for Earth, some of the interplanetary tribesmen did not. These were the Annunakis. The Annunakis for their own ego, greed and satisfaction, decided to infiltrate, or you might say, visit Earth in its earliest domain of development and instead of being implants for a Nirvanic society of high intelligence, they implanted themselves as seeds of destruction. The Annunakis are not the same intelligent life forms as the Reptilians. They are completely different, and from a different and more removed solar-based system. The Annunakis set up hostile camps in your world and over time have altered mankind's intended journey, a journey that was to have been a planetary journal of human experience devoid of war, famine, greed, and lust. Instead, the Annunakis sank the consciousness of the human experience. They have played a large role in the unseen spiritual battle to which I have referred. The Annunakis influence was first felt in the river belt region of the Tigress River, but then spread to all other continents.

That is why today, if a traveler wished to visit the Tigress or the Ganges Rivers they would find great areas of great pestilence and pride. If one were to try to recognize an intelligent form like the Annunakis, they would be looking for a humanoid form towering nearly eight feet in height and outweighing the human man form by hundreds of pounds. Some tribes of the Annunakis still inhabit your world. The Red Planet however, their original solar home, is sinking. By this, I mean, that the Red Planet is dying and it will continue to die until it can no longer sustain the Annunakis civilization, if you wish to imagine their world being civilized. Why is the Red Planet continuing its dissent and eventual disruption and extinction? Thank the Star Nation tribesmen for one. Thank the Star Galaxy, the Jupitarians, Atlanteas and Pleiadians also. For they are responsible for the eventual sinking of the Red Planet. Amen.

Time Travel

Are you aware by now that your world is spinning faster than ever before? This means that things a soul desires will be easier to manifest, quicker to manifest than in any other time in mankind's earthly history. You see things like the Bubonic Plague, Cholera, Malaria, Dysentery, Black Death, Leprosy and so many other diseases that have affected mankind over the ages were at a result of slow moving or said another way, negative energy which is dense and vibrates at a slower speed. Negativity is a very heavy and slow moving energy/frequency so the cosmos is actually healing herself; by putting elements into motion so that Mother Earth, along with the other planets, is vibrating so quickly that only the highest frequencies are in existence. With this energy in place, it will be calm, easier for mankind to travel in time. Perhaps images of young boys reading paperback books filled with images of spaceship and time travel come to your mind; this is the reality that will come into being in the decades after 2012. Stop and think about this for a moment please.

Time travel, what does it mean to you? To many souls, it means projecting one's self to a time in the far distant past or the far distant future. Both of these realities will be one. Both of these will be real possibilities, so that souls who wish to return to the slave trade in China hundreds of years ago may do so for the purpose of righting this wrong. It means that those who wish to help plant colonies on other planets for the purpose of extending greenhouses, may do so. It means that those who wish to go back to any time in earthly history where there was low consciousness demonstrated by fighting, killing, unrest, may do so with the purpose of correcting this energy, for the purpose of raising this energy to its highest most enlightened state of being.

You may be thinking that everyone will want to go back in time or forward in time but this is simply not true. Only those who carry the highest frequency within them through their thinking will be able to make the transition energetically. This is not to be confused with astral traveling or astral projection. The experience may be similar but the intention is completely different. Human souls were evolved enough upon creation to astral travel within the womb. For those unfamiliar, astral traveling is an experience where the soul projects itself into another dimension. This will continue. To repeat, time traveling is different where the intention within a soul who chooses to time travel will be in their purpose to right a wrong, recalibrate energies, provide new matrices and grids, in some cases, reformulate the genetic codes of that particular time and place. I hope that you come to view this wisdom as exciting, propelling your thoughts into the magnificent realm of infinite possibilities.

You have my permission to sign up NOW!

There will be some who will come to me directly and ask to which place they should go. To which I will respond to any place where they know there was a great deal of sadness, illness, blood loss, bigotry, persecution, either spiritual or moral and from there use their abilities to erase the cellular consciousness forever more. If you, dear souls, are of the age where it will not personally affect, know that your children's children will know it.

There is a divine intelligence, which will continue to guide and orchestrate everything involved with interstellar time travel. Mankind will simply be evolving himself or should I say within himself. Mother Earth will continue to provide her bounty for generations to come, though her soil has been tainted by these low frequencies through mankind's actions. She is a magnificent goddess who will continue to provide. Your Earth is not simply going to disappear but she will actually be restored to her previous glory.

Geometrics and Matrixes

I think it would be appropriate now to educate your minds about geometrics and matrices since these words were bought up in our discussion of time travel. You may say, "Why Angel, this seems so simplified. I know what a matrix is. I know what geometrics are." I say to you, maybe you do, maybe you don't. I would like to describe geometrics as they relate to the magnetic field because no discussion of Mother Earth can be fully complete without a discussion of geometrics and the matrix or the grid.

Two things about geometrics and how it will come upon your wisdom and how it will be shown in future generations' lives—one, the word *geometrics* will become a household word like Global Positioning Systems (GPS) have become and two, it will be demonstrated in future generations in their daily activities and here's how. If you are imagining in the next decade of the world I am trying to create within your minds, many connections between people will be expanded due to geometrics. Geometric is another word for magnetism and magnetic fields are at the core of Mother Earth; then you dear souls are an extension of a magnetic pattern. What I am trying to say is that your human DNA through its restructuring to the fifth dimension will allow a soul to be more connected. You might be asking, "To what? To God? To my neighbor? My wife? To what, Angel?" And I say to all of these things and more. No longer is the world going to be seen as co-centric; it will be viewed as *geo*centric – *geo* meaning many.

The benefits of living in a time when a person's DNA has been either genetically altered to be in the fifth dimension or revised to be Ascension energy means that in essence every individual will have the magnetic ability or the geocentric ability to communicate with anyone or everyone telepathically in any dimension, in any reality. Stop and think about that now*; in any dimension, in any reality.*

This will be particularly true for the lives of the Children of the Indigo, Crystalline and Atlantean (from Atlantis) Children. The implications for this statement are globally huge. Let me give you an example to demonstrate what I am talking about. Let me say, near the year 2020 there is a teenage boy who lives in Southern France and this teenage boy dreams of becoming an Interstellar Pilot being able to help communities, colonies trade in a galactic magnificence. He will no longer be trapped by his earthly reality; instead, he will be able to simply project through his mind to the Pleiadian Galaxy for example, if that is the galaxy of his choosing and make this happen. If it is not 2020, it will be 2030 and 2040 and 2050. Imagine getting in your car and picking up your briefcase and going into work down the street, but in actuality, you grab an interstellar vehicle, connect with another higher intelligent life form and do your work from that vantage point. It will be.

Futuristic talk such as this is not in any way shape or fashion meant to frighten or cause anxiety; it is simply an acknowledgement of the continuing shifting energies that will continue to breathe life into the human consciousness experience. This is no different really of the discovery of new planets, which is being done every day in your world. The universes are total creative storefronts if you will, that never stop creating and evolving. This is evolution to which I am speaking not fear fantasy. If mankind had stopped evolving, you would be on four legs right now. The only real difference is that future generations will have an earthly vessel or bodies, which will allow them to more easily, make the transition between dimensions. Remember time is simply a dimension.

Shifting over into matrices, who can answer the question -What is a matrix? Because part of my purpose is not only *inspiring* one's mind but also expanding it. The matrix I would like to explore right now relates to the energy of 2012. From my vantage point, many times, I view your dimension as a matrix system; some would say a very complex matrix system. Matrix simply means grid or organizational grid.

Matrix is a way of organizing energy; in your world there are earthly matrices, there are matrices from the Sirian Galaxy and the Pleiadian Galaxy, two other galaxies of which we have been speaking (of course there are others). Therefore, the matrix of your world will be strengthening by the energy of 2012. If you can imagine an unseen energy current, a very structured one that wraps your world Mother Earth in a net, this is the matrix. The matrix is sort of like the connecting fibers between the human bone and the human muscle, sometimes known as or called membrane; though the matrix is like the human membrane it plays a vital role in how things perform.

Without healthy connecting tissues, your human body will not be functioning efficiently and so it is with the matrix. Prior to 2012 the matrix grid had dissolved in places particularly in parts of the world where the conscious energy was very low, South Africa, Belfast, Northern Ireland, Pakistan, parts of India and Haiti. Almost like a pair of socks worn too long with thinning heels, this is what the matrix has looked like to me and those in my realm. In other places of the matrix, before 2012 there holes, other places of the matrix if you are imaging of this, would have brakes or pieces of the energy grid missing. I am speaking globally now, not individually, but it was the collective human consciousness, which created these maladies; all of these I just described are maladies.

A unified field is one that is restored, restructured, renewed to its original perfection that was the matrix or the grid which the God force, the Infinite Mind, created upon creation, which mankind's ignorance disturbed. With the arrival of 2012 and the years thereafter, the matrix will be restored to its original divine order with no holes, no fragments missing, no thinning of the holographic connections. This was mandatory for mankind's future survival. Now would be a good time to offer praise to whatever source you wish to thank for this loving and benevolent gift.

Dimensions

At this time, it might be appropriate and interesting to mention briefly, how the fifth dimension differs from the sixth; how the sixth differentiates from the seventh, how the seventh is differentiated from the eights and the eighth from the ninth. There are additional dimensions after the ninth and these too, will be examined at some point in time. This is largely based upon my desire to help create a text for the understanding of the majority of souls. Some of the concepts that define the tenth through the twentieth dimensions or galaxies can be complex and obscure at the same time. In so doing, it may be wise for me to describe these lower dimensions with different adjectives, because the human mind likes labels yet many of these dimensions archaracterized by conceptualism that far outreaches the human genome at this time.

To restate, it is my intention to create a document that communicates wisdom easily so that the wisdom can be spread easily from person to person, city to city, country to country. If I chose to speak in Swahili, and yet no one around me knows Swahili, then what would I have accomplished?

Let us proceed with descriptions of the fourth, fifth, sixth, seventh, eighth, and nine galaxies in understandable terms—

- Fourth Dimension—Ego, co-centric, linear, toxinated;
- Fifth Dimension—Absence of ego, absence of self, angelic in frequency and resonance, peace, love and harmony;
- Sixth Dimension—Greater extension of the Fifth;
- Seventh Dimension—The ruling energy of this dimension is harmonic frequency;
- Eight Dimension—Can be characterized as a dimension recognized by interstellar warfare, demonic interferences and capitulation. Capitulations in the sense here can be seen as overthrow. In this dimension, there is quite a bit of chaos and overthrow between galaxies;
- Ninth Dimension—Pure and total oneness.

I suppose the important truth in which I desire to communicate here is for your mind to be open to the idea that there are many realities and that more time and effort and research will be put into exploring and understanding these realities after the pinnacle of 2012 has passed. There will be a bridging of the gap between the fifth dimension and the sixth, seventh, eighth and ninth.

Q: Any information Michael, on Chiron, a comet with a unique and erratic orbit, who is symbolized in the natal chart after the 'wounded healer'?

A: Chiron is one of the newest heavenly bodies, celestial forces eighth, ninth, and tenth dimensional frequency consciousness gaining strength and momentum. Chiron is actually a collection of planets and clusters from these dimensions, not purely a comet. To some, it may seem as though I have just said something in contradiction to what they have been taught, that dimensions are clearly delineated. There is a fourth dimension and a fifth dimension clearly defined as we have been speaking about for much of this text, but when I speak about Chiron, understand please that its effects, its intelligence, extends to the eighth, ninth, and tenth galaxies. If you can imagine a ladder that takes consciousness from one level to another that is what Chiron is in place for. Chiron is a ladder of consciousness.

Chiron

Chiron has a system of leaders and intelligences all of its own. As in earthly history when there were Greek Gods and Goddesses, there are also Greek Gods and Goddesses in the essence of Chiron. As the planetary influences of Chiron continue to expand, there are certain personal characteristics that much of mankind will be able to witness within themselves. Chiron's other purpose, in addition to serving as a ladder connecting these multi-dimensions, is to smooth out any disharmonies in the human body fields. This is not as easy as it may sound, for the evolution of mankind's energy fields has gotten off track

It's a bit like a rocket that has misfired and has ended up in the South Pole instead of the North Pole. The North Pole is total oneness. The South Pole is the absence of oneness. There are a great many unseen multi-dimensional beings in my awareness and so far, I have only touched upon a few. Without hesitation, I will say that the more one wants to know about the galactic evolution in the years to come, the more readily available the information will be. Before long, many of you will be drawn like water pouring from a giant vessel, into the fields and interests of space technology, interstellar travel and communication, space stations, satellite frequency repair, harmonic convergence and further genome development. Why? Because much of what has been holding back the global population from doing so up until now is being removed. What I am trying to indicate is that in future generations the intelligence level of humankind will be greater than it has ever been.

I feel that it is important to educate those who don't know what goes on in the fifth dimension where I often dwell, to do so now. For all ears of all earthly religions, the truths that I am about to utter are truths for all men throughout all time. When a soul spark decides to incarnate and enter the fourth dimension, your realm, they must make the transition for the fifth dimension to the fourth. In my mind, this is the biggest, most profound act of creation ever known! Think of it this way please—the spark of every soul that passes through a lower frequency dimension must slow itself/the particle/the essence down so much that the essence of a soul spark can become a human bodily form. It is a molecular change of enormous proportions! Let me say this another way…if you can imagine the highest frequency of electricity, a Crystalline beam, that beam exists in a dimension where there is nothing but love and light and goodness, acceptance, wisdom, truth, joy and compassion, and at some point, this spark with its own intelligence, this bit of electrify if you will, chooses to slow its vibration down enough to become solid matter. This is the miracle of creation, the miracle of life as it begins in the fifth dimension!

If you are following, I am talking about earthly life; life in other dimensions begins in other dimensions; the fifth dimension is where all of the great masters often reside. It is the dimension where the angelic and divine realm exists. Imagine in your mind the most loving, the most sacred, the most beautiful feeling that you have ever felt and I say to you, this is from where you originated and this is where 2012 will take you again!

When a soul decides to end their earthly journey in the body vessel known as man or woman, they ascend back to the fifth dimension and the miraculous process of rebirth, reformation, begins all over again. The spiritual wisdom contained here is that once something is created it can never be destroyed. It can change form, but it can never be destroyed. You might find it fun to view the universe as the great Mulligan Stew in the sky. It can be said that there are many impurities in thought creation that float around in space. These thought impurities have given rise to civilizations, nomadic in nature, rising and falling much like the civilizations on your Earth. You see, there is divine wisdom even in this. There is sort of a filtering system to catch the dust, the toxins, the unused particles of thought energy, so the multi-universes can run as smoothly as a well-tuned automobile. Imagine now that every thought created is an energy statement and that it is stored and housed in either the fifth, sixth, or seventh dimension, to be dissected, improved and rebirthed later. What would you say? It is true. You might call it the cosmic tune up.

6

Final Angelic Thoughts

As mankind's consciousness continues to evolve and his thoughts become more pure, less toxic, less poisoned, there will be less and less need for the systems that have been put into place to cleanse them. The mind of the multi-realities is really almost too great to comprehend. This to me is what God/Infinite Mind is. As you fall asleep tonight many of you saying your silent prayers or giving offerings to Mother Nature, to the leaders of your faith, or to yourselves, I ask you to remember this final bit of wisdom before I leave you—love is invincible, love is everlasting, love knows no boundaries. The vibration of love was responsible for creating the planet Earth and it is to this consciousness frequency that your world will be restored to in 2012 and beyond.

Be blessed, rejoice, celebrate the coming years as a set of the most fortunate of most fortunate circumstances in which to witness.

I hope that I have helped you. —*Michael*

About the Author

KELLY HAMPTON IS RAPIDLY BECOMING ONE OF THE TOP visionaries in the world of psychic mediums, angelic channels, energy healers, spiritual authors and teachers. She has been lecturing and giving divine guidance for over twenty years, helping guide and educate thousands of people on topics related to channeling, healing of the body and mind, development of intuition, connecting with angels and more recently the spiritual truths of 2012. She has become an expert guest on many Blog Talk Radio programs. She is currently at work facilitating workshops in Star Healing Intergalactic Energy™, a new groundbreaking healing modality that was revealed comprehensively to her by Archangel Michael in January 2010 for the Ascension.

Her first book, **Into the White Light: The Revelations of Archangel Michael** was given to her in 2004 from her divine source and continues to be profoundly important in helping people understanding and expand their spiritual wisdom. She is grateful to be the messenger and as Archangel Michael has expressed time and time again, "2012 is the time of the Great Awakening, the time of the Great Shift in Consciousness, the time when light overcomes darkness." Please contact Kelly at www. IntoTheWhiteLight.com or call 636-346-7093 for further information on her work. Follow her on Facebook, YouTube, Twitter and other social media.